LOVE VEGAN

The Essential Christmas Cookbook for Vegans

Zoe Hazan

HIGH CEDAR PRESS

LOVE VEGAN

The Essential Christmas Cookbook for Vegans

High Cedar Press

Copyright © 2017

Kindle Edition

Published by High Cedar Press

Illustrations Copyright © 2017

DISCLAIMER

TThe full contents of 'Love Vegan', including text, comments, graphics, images, and other content are for informational purposes only. The information is not intended to diagnose, treat, cure or prevent any illnesses or diseases. Always consult you physician before changing dietary habits.

'Love Vegan' does not provide specific information or advice regarding food intolerance or allergies. It is the responsibility of the reader to ensure any diagnosed or potential food intolerances are identified and excluded from the recipes.

The author and publisher make no guarantee as to the availability of ingredients mentioned in this book. Many ingredients vary in size and texture and these differences may affect the outcome of some recipes. The author has tried to make the recipes as accurate and workable as possible, however, cannot be responsible for any recipe not working.

Every effort has been made to prepare this material to ensure it's accuracy, however, the author nor publisher will be held responsible if there is information deemed as inaccurate.

CONTENTS

• •

DESSERTS & TREATS

INTRODUCTION

Discover vegan versions of the warm and rich comforting food we all look forward to over the holidays. Whether you're a mince pie fan or a full-on gingerbread fiend, Love Vegan has the perfect recipe for you. Prepare yourself for a world of recipes that are full of spices, mouth-watering aromas, and festive flavors - all cooked with ease in your very own kitchen.

Love Vegan: Christmas Made Easy features delicious vegan recipes perfectly suited for a traditional Christmas experience, all of which can be prepared in less than 30 minutes using simple and easy to follow instructions suitable for even the most inexperienced cook.

As we all know Christmas is a time to get the family together, to give presents and (most importantly) to feast on festive dishes. Just because you are vegan that doesn't mean you should miss out on all the culinary joy this day has to offer.

This cookbook offers recipes which are made with easy to source ingredients. So not only you will spend little time preparing, but you will not have to run around looking for expensive specialty ingredients.

From Creamy Christmas Eggnog to moreish Mince Pies, and even luxurious centerpieces such as Mushroom Wellington with Red Wine Gravy, you really will be spoiled for choice. This book offers a fantastic selection of vegan alternatives to everyone's favorites dishes, from starters to desserts.

Let our holiday recipes inspire you this year, whether you are feeding a crowd of hungry vegans or cooking just for yourself, this book will help make the occasion really special and ensure you are not missing out.

This cookbook series aims to shed some light on the vegan lifestyle and health benefits that will follow. We believe that whatever your reasons are for integrating vegan food into your diet the end result should be full of flavor and authenticity.

Whether you are a vegan, a vegetarian or a meat-eater looking to reduce the amount of meat based meals in your diet, this book can help inspire you to cook indulgent, delicious and satisfying meals to make this a Christmas to remember.

Christmas only comes once a year but with these mouth-watering recipes you will wish it were more often!

Merry Christmas all!

MAINS

LENTIL & MUSHROOM ROAST
WITH ONION GRAVY

This filling and delicious roast is the perfect centerpiece for your vegan Christmas table and a great alternative to meat. It complements the traditional Christmas trimmings and side dishes and is easy to make. Serve with lashings of flavorsome onion gravy!

Preparation Time
15 minutes

Total Time
60 minutes

Makes
6 servings

INGREDIENTS

FOR THE LENTIL LOAF

1 tbsp olive oil
1 small red onion, finely chopped
3 cloves garlic, minced
1 celery stick, finely chopped
8 chestnut / button mushrooms, finely chopped
1 medium carrot, peeled & grated
1 can kidney beans, rinsed & drained
1 can puy lentils, rinsed & drained
1 tbsp soy sauce
1 tsp dried parsley
1 tsp dried basil
1 tsp oregano

½ tsp thyme
4 tbsp nutritional yeast
½ tsp black pepper
¾ tsp salt
140g/ 1½ cups rolled oats

FOR THE ONION GRAVY

1 vegetable stock cube + ½ litre / 2 cups boiling water
1 medium red onion, finely chopped
2 tbsp olive oil
1 tbsp brown sugar
1 tbsp cornflour or tapioca powder
7oz / 200ml vegan red wine
2 tbsp balsamic vinegar
3 tbsp soy sauce

DIRECTIONS

TO MAKE THE LENTIL LOAF:

Preheat oven to 350° and line a loaf tin with parchment paper. Heat the oil in a large pan and sauté the onions for 5 minutes until soft. Add the garlic and cook for a minute. Add the mushroom, celery, and carrots and cook for around 5-7 minutes until soft, then mix in the rest of the loaf ingredients until well combined.

Mash the ingredients together using either a potato masher or a fork until it all comes together but make sure to not over mash. You want there to be lots of texture. Add 1 tbsp more oats if the mixture is too wet or 1 tbsp more water if the mixture is too dry.

Carefully transfer into the loaf tin and use the back of a spoon to smooth the top. Bake in the oven for 40-45 minutes until the top is firm.

TO MAKE THE GRAVY:

While the loaf is in the oven you can prepare the gravy.

Place the stock cube in ½ litre of boiling water, give it a good stir and set aside.

Heat oil in a frying pan and sauté the onions for 10 minutes. Add the brown sugar and fry for 5 minutes until caramelized. Add the cornflour / tapioca flour and mix well. Cook for 1-2 minutes, stirring constantly to avoid the onions burning or sticking to the pan.

Pour in the wine, balsamic and soy sauce and simmer on a low heat for 10 minutes, stirring frequently until the liquid has reduced by half.

Add the stock and allow the liquid to simmer again for 10-15 minutes until the gravy has thickened and become nice and glossy.

You can set this aside and simply reheat once the lentils are ready, or even prepare this up to 1 day ahead. If you are making the gravy in advance allow it cool down to room temperature, then keep in the fridge in an airtight container until you are ready to serve.

MUSHROOM WELLINGTON
WITH RED WINE GRAVY

You can't go wrong with this impressive and elegant dish that is surprisingly easy to make. Soft and tender mushrooms are encased in beautiful vegan puff pastry and drizzled with a rich and luxurious red wine gravy.

Preparation Time
25 minutes

Total Time
1 hour 25 minutes

Makes
2 servings

INGREDIENTS

FOR THE MUSHROOM WELLINGTON

1 sheet vegan puff pastry
4 portobello mushrooms
3.5oz / 100g shiitake mushrooms
3.5oz / 100g button mushrooms
2 cup spinach, washed
3 shallots, roughly chopped
3 garlic cloves, minced
2 sprigs rosemary

½ tsp fresh thyme
1 tbsp fresh parsley, chopped
¼ tsp freshly ground pepper
¼ tsp salt
Olive oil for greasing

FOR THE RED WINE GRAVY

½ cup red wine
1 ½ cups vegetable stock
¼ tsp ground black pepper
1 tbsp all-purpose flour
2 tbsp olive oil

DIRECTIONS

Preheat the oven to 400°. Grease a baking tray with a little olive oil.

To start, place the portobello mushrooms on a cutting board and remove the stem, then gently scrape out the gills on the underside using a spoon, being careful not to break or tear the mushroom. Place on baking tray and bake in the oven for 10 minutes. Once cooked transfer to a plate and set aside. Keep the oven on but reduce the heat to 370°. Wipe the baking tray and line with parchment paper.

FOR THE FILLING:

In a food processor or blender add spinach, shallots, shitake and button mushrooms, garlic, herbs and seasoning, and pulse in short bursts until the mixture is finely chopped yet coarse, being careful not to over process the mixture as you do not want a puree. Transfer to a medium bowl and set aside.

TO MAKE THE WELLINGTONS:

Allow the pastry to come to room temperature for 10 minutes before using it. Using a sharp knife or pizza cutter divide pastry sheet into 4 equal parts. Place a portobello mushroom in the center of the piece, cavity side up, and fill with ¼ of the mushroom-spinach filling. Continue with remaining pastry quarters, portobello mushrooms and filling.

Gently fold pastry around mushroom and ensure it is fully sealed, using your fingers to pinch pastry together to enclose all edges.

Transfer all mushroom wellingtons to the baking tray and bake in the pre-heated oven for 25-27 minutes or until the pastry is golden brown.

FOR THE RED WINE GRAVY:

While the wellingtons are in the oven you can make the gravy. In a small saucepan heat add olive oil over medium heat and once hot add flour, whisking constantly for 1-2 minutes. Pour in red wine, pepper, and stock and bring to a boil. Reduce to a simmer and cook uncovered for 20 minutes or until it has thickened and become the consistency of a rich gravy. Transfer to a gravy dish.

Serve all when piping hot with vegetables and drizzle gravy over the wellington.

.

CHESTNUT MUSHROOM BOURGUIGNON

The traditional beef bourguignon gets a vegan makeover with this delicious mushroom version. A crowd pleasing meal that features a rich and savory red wine gravy and best of all you don't need to braise it for hours making this a great weeknight dish for those cold winter nights.

Preparation Time
10 minutes

Total Time
5 minutes

Makes
4 servings

INGREDIENTS

2 tbsp olive oil
4.5oz / 130g shallots, chopped
8.8oz / 250g Chantenay carrots
2 large cloves garlic, minced
1lb / 450g Chestnut / Crimini mushrooms
7oz / 200g Portobello mushrooms

3 tbsp all-purpose flour, sieved
1 ½ cups / 375ml vegan red wine
1 ¼ cups / 300ml vegetable stock
2 tbsp tomato purée
1 tsp fresh thyme or ½ tsp dried
Salt and pepper, to tastel

DIRECTIONS

To start, clean the mushrooms and cut them all into quarters or slices if you prefer. Half the carrots lengthways and set aside.

Heat oil in a large dutch oven or heavy-bottomed saucepan over medium high heat. Add the shallots and saute for 5 minutes until they have softened. Add the carrots and garlic and fry for 2 minutes then add all of the mushrooms and seasoning and stir for 2 minutes until they begin to darken but have not released too much liquid, around 1 minute.

Sieve the flour into the pan and continue to stir for a minute until all the mushrooms are coated.

Pour in the red wine, bring to a rolling boil for a minute then reduce to a vigorous simmer and allow the wine to reduce for 2-3 minutes. Add the stock, tomato purée, and thyme and cook over medium high heat for 15-20 minutes until you have a thick and glossy sauce.

Serve immediately over potato or swede mash.

STUFFED SEITAN ROAST

This savory and festive meat-free roast makes a fabulous centrepiece for the holidays. This roast would be perfect served at the Christmas table and would satisfy vegans, vegetarians and meat eaters alike. The only ingredient that may be a little hard to find is vital wheat gluten - which cannot be substituted for another type of flour, however it can be easily sourced online.

Preparation Time
30 minutes

Total Time
1 hour 30 minutes

Makes
4 servings

INGREDIENTS

FOR THE FILLING:

1 tbsp olive oil
1 large red onion, finely chopped
2 cloves garlic, finely chopped
½ cup mushrooms, chopped
1 tbsp soy sauce
6oz / 175g chopped apple
1 ½ oz / 40g prunes, chopped
½ can (4oz / 120g) kidney beans
1oz / 25g walnuts, finely chopped
1 tsp vegan bouillon
3 tbsp fresh parsley, chopped
¼ tsp salt
½ tsp black pepper

FOR THE SEITAN:

6oz / 175g vital wheat gluten flour
1 tsp garlic powder
1 tsp onion powder
1 tsp dried oregano
½ tsp dried rosemary
½ tsp dried thyme
2 heaped tbsp nutritional yeast
2 tbsp soy sauce
1 tsp liquid smoke (optional)
1 cup / 250ml vegetable stock
½ can (4 oz / 120g) kidney beans
1 tbsp tomato puree

DIRECTIONS

TO MAKE THE FILLING:

Heat olive oil in a large skillet and saute onions for 5-6 minutes until soft. Add the garlic and mushrooms and cook until the mushrooms have released most of their liquid. Add the soy sauce, apples, prunes, drained and rinsed kidney beans, walnuts, and stock powder and cook for 5 minutes, stirring frequently. Remove from the heat and roughly mash the filling with the fork or a potato masher, ensuring most of the beans are mashed. Set aside.

TO MAKE THE SEITAN:

Preheat the oven to 350 F°.

In a large bowl combine the flour, garlic powder, onion powder, oregano, rosemary, thyme, and nutritional yeast. Set aside.

Pour soy sauce, liquid smoke, vegetable stock, drained and rinsed kidney beans, and tomato puree into a blender and pulse until smooth.

Pour the liquid into the flour mixture and stir until the dough starts to come together. Knead for 2-3 minutes until you have a soft dough.

Place a large piece of plastic on your kitchen counter. Roll the seitan out over the plastic wrap, or use your hands to spread it out into a rectangular shape (approx. 10x12"), making sure it is the same thickness in all places. You may prefer to place another piece of plastic wrap onto the top of the dough (so it is sandwiched between the two) to make rolling easier. Once rolled out check for any holes and pinch the dough together to repair any you see.

Spread the stuffing evenly over the dough, leaving a 2" margin around the edges. Use the plastic wrap to roll the roast as tightly as possible by lifting the plastic wrap on one of the long edges and roll it like a large swiss roll. Pinch the long seal to ensure the stuffing will not leak, then pinch both ends to securely close them.

Place a large sheet of aluminum foil on your kitchen counter and grease with a little olive oil. Carefully transfer the seitan from the plastic wrap onto the aluminum foil and wrap it tightly around the roast, twisting both ends to seal them.

Bake in the preheated oven for 60 minutes, turning the roast every 20 minutes to ensure it cooks evenly.

Remove from the oven and leave the seitan to cool for 15-20 minutes before serving.

This is a great make ahead meal as the roast can be prepared a day in advance and kept in the fridge once it has cooled down to room temperature.

Keep it in the foil and heat in a preheated oven for 10-15 minutes.

STUFFED BUTTERNUT ROAST

This vibrant and exciting butternut squash is a great way to enjoy wonderful winter veggies and will impress vegans and carnivores alike. It is packed full of rich and hearty flavors and is a great crowd pleaser.

Preparation Time	**Total Time**	**Makes**
15 minutes	1 hour 5 minutes	4 servings

INGREDIENTS

1 large butternut squash
2 tbsp olive oil
1 small red onion, finely chopped
2 cloves garlic, minced
3.5oz / 100g puy lentils
2.4oz / 70g cranberries
1oz / 30g sultanas
2 sprigs rosemary, finely chopped
2 stalks thyme, leaves removed
½ tsp freshly grated nutmeg or 1 tsp ground nutmeg
½ cup + 3 tbsp / 150ml vegan red wine
½ cup + 3 tbsp / 150ml vegetable stock
2.8oz / 80g fresh spinach, finely chopped
1.7oz / 50g walnuts, roughly chopped

DIRECTIONS

IPreheat the oven to 350° F.

Slice the butternut squash lengthways as evenly as possible and remove the seeds.

Coat both sides with 1 tbsp of olive oil then bake for 35-40 minutes or until the flesh is soft and tender. Remove from the oven and set aside.

In a large pan or pot with a lid, heat the oil and sauté the onions for 5 minutes then add the garlic, stirring for a minute.

Mix in the remaining ingredients, except for the spinach and walnuts Bring to a boil, then cover and reduce to a low simmer.

Cook for 30 minutes until the lentils are tender but not mushy. Check the mixture during the last 10 minutes as you may need to add a dash more water to prevent it from drying out. At the very end of the cooking time add the spinach and stir well so that the heat allows it to wilt.

Preheat the oven to 350° F.

Very carefully scoop out the flesh from the butternut squash, being very careful not to tear the skin. You could use a very sharp knife to cut around ½ - 1 inch from the skin, making it easier to remove the flesh. Add to the lentils and mash it in with a fork, mixing well. Stir in the walnuts.

Spoon the mixture into both halves of the squash until it is level but be sure not to overfill. There is likely to be leftover filling which you can refrigerate and use another time.

Place one-half on top of the other and carefully tie with a string. Do not pull the strings too tight or the filling will start to pour out of the sides, but ensure it is secured enough to prevent it coming apart.

Return to the oven for 10 minutes. Remove and serve immediately while hot.

LUXURY NUT ROAST

This satisfying and filling nut roast is packed with nuts, pulses, and spices. A nut roast is most commonly served during the holidays in replace of a meat-based meal, however, this delicious and easy-to-make vegan version can be enjoyed at any time of the year.

Preparation Time	Total Time	Makes
15 minutes	1 hour	4 servings

INGREDIENTS

1 cup mixed nuts, roughly chopped
1 cup cooked or tinned lentils (green or brown)
2 small onions, finely chopped
2 large garlic cloves, minced
1 large carrots, grated
1 large celery stick, finely chopped
1 ½ cup breadcrumbs

1 tbsp soy sauce
1 tsp ground cumin
1 tsp turmeric
1 tsp ground coriander
¼ tsp cayenne pepper
1 tbsp cornflour + 2 tbsp water
¼ tsp coarse salt
½ tsp ground black pepper
Vegetable oil, for frying

DIRECTIONS

Preheat the oven to 350°. Grease a loaf tin with a little olive oil and set aside.

Heat oil in a large saucepan and sauté onions, carrot and celery for 4-5 minutes until soft. Add garlic, all the spices and soy sauce and fry for a minute. Stir in lentils and nuts then transfer to a large mixing bowl.

In a small bowl combine cornflour with water and stir until dissolved. Pour into lentil mixture and stir well until fully combined. Fold in breadcrumbs then transfer to the loaf tin. Using the back of a spoon press the mixture firmly into the tin and smooth over the top.

Bake in the oven for 45 minutes. Leave to set for 5-10 minutes before serving.

Serve with gravy.

SEED & CARROT LOAF

This super healthy loaf is totally gluten free, wheat free and dairy free, making it a nutritious main course to serve over the holidays. The loaf is beautifully moist with a lovely texture produced by the sunflower and pumpkin seeds. It makes a wonderful main dish served with roast potatoes, gravy and veg!

Preparation Time	**Total Time**	**Makes**
25 minutes	1 hour 10 minutes	4 servings

INGREDIENTS

3 large carrots, unpeeled & chopped
150g / 1 cup sunflower seeds, ground
150g / 1 cup pumpkin seeds, ground
1 tbsp spelt flour
½ tbsp soy sauce

3 cloves garlic, crushed
1 tbsp fresh rosemary, chopped
1 tbsp fresh parsley, chopped
1 tbsp fresh basil, chopped
1 tsp ground black pepper
1 tsp coarse salt

* If you are unable to source fresh herbs you can use ½ tbsp each of dried.

DIRECTIONS

IPreheat the oven to 400°F and line an 8 x 4 loaf tin with parchment paper.

Cook the carrots until soft by either boiling or steaming them. Mash completely until they turn into a pulp then set aside.

In a large bowl mix all ingredients together very well. Mix for around 1-2 minutes to ensure everything is well combined.

Pour the mixture into the loaf tin and use the back of a spoon to firmly press down, using a good amount of pressure. If you do not press hard enough the loaf will fall apart when you serve it.

Bake for 45 minutes then leave in the tin for 5 minutes before removing and slicing.

CARAMELISED ONION TART TATIN

Impress your guests with this savory version of a classic French dish. Red and white onions are caramelised until sweet and sticky and then baked to perfection in a flakey pastry crust. This tart is a great centrepiece and can be served with a simple salad or steamed vegetables.

Preparation Time
15 minutes

Total Time
1 hour 10 minutes

Makes
4 servings.

INGREDIENTS

1.7oz / 50g vegan butter
2 medium yellow onions, peeled & halved
1 medium red onion, peeled & halved
2 tbsp agave nectar or maple syrup

2 tbsp balsamic vinegar
2 sprigs fresh rosemary
Salt & freshly ground black pepper
8.8oz / 250g homemade or store bought vegan puff pastry

DIRECTIONS

Preheat the oven to 350°.

Heat an 8" heavy-bottomed skillet (approx 2" deep) with butter over medium heat.

Add the onion halves, cut side up and fry for 5 minutes, carefully shaking the pan to prevent the onions from sticking to the bottom. Gently turn the onion over and fry for another 7 minutes. Add the maple syrup and vinegar and cook for a minute. Remove from the heat, cover with a lid or carefully seal with foil and bake in the oven for 20 minutes.

Remove the skillet from the oven and allow to cool slightly while preparing the pastry. Arrange the onions neatly in the skillet as you will be inverting the tart when serving.

Lay the pre-rolled pastry onto a lightly floured surface and cut a circle slightly larger in diameter than the skillet (approx. 32"). Pierce all over with a fork then place the pastry over the onions and tuck it in around the sides of the pan, encasing the onions.

Bake for 20-25 minutes until the pastry has risen and is golden brown. Leave to stand for 5 minutes before turning the skillet over onto a plate and turning upside down to release it.

Serve warm or cold with a side salad.

VEGAN HAGGIS

A haggis recipe with the flavor, spices, and texture of a conventional haggis - except it is totally meat free! This vegan haggis is made with pearl barley to provide a lovely 'meaty' texture and flavoured with wonderful festive spices.

Preparation Time
30 minutes

Total Time
1 hour 10 minutes

Makes
4-6 servings

INGREDIENTS

2 tbsp olive oil
3.5 oz / 100g brown or green lentils
2.5 oz / 75g pearl barley
1 large onion, finely chopped
2 cloves garlic, crushed
1 rib of celery, finely chopped
1 large carrot, peeled & finely chopped
3.5 oz / 100g chestnut mushrooms, finely chopped
½ tsp ground allspice
½ tsp ground nutmeg

½ tsp ground mace
3.5 oz / 100g rolled oats
2.4 oz / 75g raw walnuts, chopped roughly
1 tsp fresh parsley, chopped or ½ tsp dried
2 tbsp soy sauce
1 tbsp brown miso paste
2 cups / 500ml vegetable stock, made with boiling water
½ tsp salt
½ tsp pepper

DIRECTIONS

Preheat the oven to 350°. Generously grease a pudding basin or oven proof dish with butter or oil and set aside.

Cook the lentils and barley in separate pots with 1 tsp of salt in each for around 20 minutes. They both want to be cooked but retain some 'bite' so ensure you stop cooking them if they get mushy. Drain and set aside.

Heat the olive oil in a large frying pan and sauté the onions for 5 minutes until soft. Add the carrot and celery and fry for 3-4 minutes until soft.

Add the mushrooms and garlic, the add the spices after a minute. Stir constantly while the mushrooms emit liquid.

Mix in the lentils and oats, combining well, then pour in the hot stock, soy sauce, and miso. Simmer over a low heat until the mixture becomes very thick, around 8-10 minutes. Add a dash more water if the mixture dries out and starts sticking to the bottom of the pan.

Pour in the pearl barley, walnuts, parsley, and seasoning and mix very well.

Transfer mixture into basin or dish, pressing down as you go along, then cover the top with foil, completely sealing any gaps. Bake for 20 minutes then remove the foil and bake for another 20 minutes.

Remove from the oven and gently run a sharp knife around the rim of the dish. Slip a plate over the end and carefully flip upright in order to remove the haggis. You may need to gently tap the dish to help it turn out.

POLENTA WITH WILD MUSHROOM & ROSEMARY CASHEW CREAM

This spectacular dish is a real show stopper and is guaranteed to impress! While the preparation may seem a little long winded, rest assured it will be well worth your time. The cashew cream and the polenta can both be made in advance reducing your workload when preparing the dish.

Preparation Time
30 minutes
(+ overnight to
soak cashews)

Total Time
45 minutes

Makes
4 servings

INGREDIENTS

FFOR THE CASHEW CREAM:

1 ½ cups cashews, soaked overnight
¾ cup water
1 tbsp lemon juice
1 tsp dijon mustard
1 ½ tbsp nutritional yeast
1 small clove garlic, finely chopped
½ tsp sea salt
¼ tsp black pepper

FOR THE MUSHROOMS:

2 small shallots, thinly sliced
1 tbsp olive oil or vegan butter
16oz / 450g wild mushrooms
2 garlic cloves, finely chopped
2 tbsp fresh sage
¼ tsp sea salt

FOR THE BAKED POLENTA:

2 ¼ cups / 530ml water
1 cup / 235ml unsweetened vegan milk
1 tbsp vegan butter
½ tsp salt
¼ tsp black pepper
6.3oz / 180g ground polenta
1 tbsp olive oil
½ tsp dried sage

¼ tsp black pepper
6 tbsp cashew cream

DIRECTIONS

TO MAKE THE CASHEW CREAM:

Drain and rinse the cashews. Place all ingredients in a high speed blender and pulse until completely smooth and creamy. Scrape down the sides as you go along. Set aside.

Combine all ingredients in a food processor. Mix for 1-2 minutes. Scrape down the sides and process again until smooth and creamy.

TO MAKE THE BAKED POLENTA:

Preheat the oven to 350 °F. Grease an 8x12" baking dish with vegan butter and set aside.

Heat water, milk, butter, salt, and pepper in a medium saucepan and bring to a boil. Add the polenta in a slow stream whisking constantly. Add the olive oil and stir frequently with a wooden spoon until thick, around 20 minutes. If you wish to reduce the cooking time you can use instant polenta which should take around 5 minutes to cook.

Remove from the heat and stir in 2 tablespoons of the cashew cream and dried sage. Pour the polenta into the greased baking tray and smooth over the top with the back of a spoon or a knife. Bake for 15 minutes.

While the polenta is baking heat a large skillet with oil or butter over medium heat and saute the shallots for 2-3 minutes then add the mushrooms, garlic, salt, and pepper and cook for 5-6 minutes or until the mushrooms have darkened and the liquid has evaporated. Remove from the heat and add the sage.

Remove the polenta from the oven and spread with 6 tablespoons of the cashew cream then top with mushrooms. Put back in the oven for 5 minutes.

Remove and let the polenta set for 5 minutes before slicing and serving with a dollop of the remaining cashew cream.

CHESTNUT & WILD MUSHROOM STRUDEL

Crispy golden filo pastry encases a simple yet delicious mushroom and chestnut filling. This is a dish that will really impress your guests as it feels luxurious and gourmet, but the truth is that it's pretty easy to make!

Preparation Time
10 minutes

Total Time
45 minutes

Makes
2-3 servings

INGREDIENTS

1 tbsp olive oil
3 shallots, finely chopped
3 cloves garlic, crushed
9 oz / 250g wild mushrooms, chopped
9 oz / 250g firm tofu
1 tbsp soy sauce
1 tsp lemon juice
2 oz / 50g ground walnuts
1 tin (13.5 oz / 390g) or dry

chestnuts, roughly chopped
2 tbsp fresh parsley leaves, chopped
1 tsp fresh or dried thyme
½ tsp salt
½ tsp pepper
1 packet (8.5 oz / 250g) vegan filo pastry
Redcurrant jelly to serve

DIRECTIONS

To start, remove tofu from packaging and press between two towels to remove excess water. You can use something weighted, such as a large saucepan or a heavy chopping board and place this on top of the tofu to squeeze out as much moisture as possible for a minimum of 10 minutes. This process will allow the tofu to absorb much more flavor.

While the tofu is being pressed heat oil in a large pan and sauté the shallots until soft, around 5 minutes. Add the garlic and mushroom along with salt and pepper and cook for 7-10 minutes or until the mushrooms release all of their liquid. Remove from heat and set aside.

Crumble the tofu into a bowl using a fork and add soy sauce, walnuts, chestnuts, parsley, thyme and cooked mushroom/shallot mixture and stir well to combine. Leave to cool down while preparing the filo pastry.

Preheat the oven to 350°F. Line a baking tray with parchment paper and grease with a little oil.

Place one piece of filo pastry on a clean work surface and gently brush with oil. Top with another pastry sheet and brush with oil again. Repeat until you have four pastry sheets stacked. Spoon $^1/_3$ of the mushroom mixture on one edge of the pastry and very carefully roll, folding the edges in as you go along and tucking in the top so you have completely encased the filling with the pastry.

Once you have a firm log with no seals carefully transfer to the baking sheet and repeat with remaining filling and filo until you have three strudels. Brush lightly with oil and sprinkle with salt and pepper.

Bake in the oven for 30 minutes until golden brown. Serve immediately with redcurrant jelly.

SIDES

GARLIC MUSHROOM PÂTÉ

This healthy and easy vegan starter is the perfect appetizer to whet your appetite before your Christmas meal. It will keep in the fridge for 1 week so you can make this ahead to reduce your workload on the day.

Preparation Time
25 minutes
(plus 1 hour for
pâté to cool)

Total Time
15 minutes

Makes
2-3 cups
(depending on
the variety of
mushrooms you
use)

INGREDIENTS

2 tbsp olive oil or vegan butter
10.5 oz / 300g mushrooms, chopped
1 cup raw cashews
2 shallots, finely chopped
5 cloves garlic, crushed

1 tsp soy sauce
2 sprigs thyme, leaves removed
½ tsp dry sherry (optional)
¼ tsp salt
¼ tsp pepper

DIRECTIONS

Heat a large frying pan and dry fry the cashews for a minute, moving them around constantly, until they are golden brown. Alternatively you can pop them in the oven at 350° for 3-4 minutes, keeping an eye on them and moving them around frequently. Remove and set aside.

Using the same frying pan (you do not need to wash it) heat the oil or butter and sauté the shallots for a few minutes until soft. Add the garlic and mushrooms and fry for 4-5 minutes until the mushrooms have softened and released some of their liquid.

Add the soy sauce, thyme, sherry, and seasoning and continue to fry until most of the liquid has evaporated, around 5 minutes.

Transfer the mushroom mixture and the roasted cashew nuts into a high-speed blender or food processor and blend until it turns into a paste. Continue to blend if you like a smooth pâté or leave it a little chunky.

Transfer to a serving dish then allow the pâté to cool to room temperature then chill in the fridge for at least an hour before serving.

CRANBERRY, WALNUT & HERB CHEESE BALL

This elegant holiday appetizer is really versatile so you can play around with different flavors and toppings. You could try sun-dried tomatoes and olives, or perhaps sultanas and pistachios. Serve with crackers and chutney for a traditional festive treat.

Preparation Time	**Total Time**	**Makes**
10 minute (+ 4 hours for cashews to soak) s	1 hour 15 minutes	6-8 servings

INGREDIENTS

1 cup raw cashews
2 tbsp freshly squeezed lemon juice
2 tbsp nutritional yeast
2 tbsp coconut oil, melted
2 tsp white miso paste
1 clove garlic, peeled & roughly chopped
¼ tsp coarse salt

1 tbsp fresh parsley, chopped
1 tbsp fresh chives, chopped
½ tsp thyme
½ tsp rosemary
½ cup dried cranberries
¼ cup walnuts, roughly chopped

DIRECTIONS

Place cashews in a heatproof bowl and cover with boiling water. Cover the bowl and leave to soak for a minimum of 4 hours, preferably overnight.

Line a small bowl with plastic wrap and set aside.

Drain the cashews and place in a food processor or high-speed blender along with lemon juice, nutritional yeast, oil, miso paste, garlic, and salt. Blend until very smooth and creamy, and no lumps remain. Add the chopped herbs, cranberries, and walnuts and pulse once or twice in short bursts to just mix the ingredients together, but be careful not to blend.

Spoon the mixture into the lined bowl and place an additional layer of plastic wrap over the top so it is sealed.

Chill for either 1 hour in the freezer or 3 hours in the fridge before serving.

The cheeseball will keep for 3-4 days, covered, in the fridge.

SPICY 'SAUSAGE' ROLLS

This recipe shows that becoming vegan doesn't mean you have to miss out on your favorite foods. Delicious juicy 'sausage' meat is encased in light crisp and flaky pastry, making this recipe perfect for any occasion.

| **Preparation Time** | **Total Time** | **Makes** |
| 10 minutes | 40 minutes | 6 'sausage' rolls |

INGREDIENTS

350g homemade or storebought puff pastry
1 can (14.1 oz / 400g) butter beans
1 can (14.1 oz / 400g) kidney beans
2 tbsp ground cumin
2 tbsp nutritional yeast
1 tsp onion powder
1 tsp garlic powder

1 tsp paprika
¾ tsp dried oregano
1 tsp red chili flakes
½ tsp cayenne pepper (optional)
3 ½ tbsp rolled porridge oats
½ tsp coarse salt
½ tsp ground black pepper
Olive oil, for greasing

DIRECTIONS

Preheat the oven to 200°/390°. Grease a baking tray with a little olive oil.

Add all of the beans to a blender along with all of the spices and pulse in short bursts until the mixture is combined. Add the oats and pulse a few more times until fully incorporated. You want the beans to have just broken down, you do not want a smooth puree.

Roll out the puff pastry into a large rectangle then cut into twelve even squares. Evenly split the filling into six, make sausage shapes then place in the center of the pastry square.

If you have any leftover bean mixture you can freeze this for later use.

Brush a little water around the edges of the pastry then lay the second sheet on top, using your fingers to gently press down to seal the edges. Slice each roll in half so you are left with six 'sausage' rolls. Make a few incisions into the pastry using a sharp knife on the top of the roll to let steam out.

Place on baking tray and bake for 20-25 minutes until the pastry has puffed up and turned golden brown.

MUSHROOM, SAGE & PINE NUT STUFFING

A savory and flavorsome stuffing that makes a fantastic replacement for a meat-based recipe. Quinoa is mixed with mushrooms, onions, and garlic, making a moist side dish for your Christmas feast.

Preparation Time	**Total Time**	**Makes**
15 minutes	30 minutes	6-8 servings

INGREDIENTS

½ cup pine nuts
1 ½ cups quinoa, uncooked and thoroughly washed
2 ½ cups water
1 tbsp olive oil
1 large onion, finely chopped
3 large garlic cloves, minced
2 sticks celery, finely chopped

4 cups mushrooms, finely chopped
2 tbsp fresh sage, chopped
½ cup vegetable stock
1 tsp salt
½ tsp ground black pepper
2 tbsp vegan butter

DIRECTIONS

Heat a medium pan and dry fry the pine nuts for 1-2 minutes until golden brown. Be sure to move them around constantly as they burn very quickly. Remove from heat and set aside.

Heat a saucepan with 2 ½ cups of water and ½ tsp salt and bring to a boil, then add the quinoa, cover, reduce to a low simmer and cook for 12-15 minutes. Remove from the heat, uncover and fluff up with a fork once cooked.

In the same pan that was used for the pine nuts (no need to wash), heat oil and sauté the onions for 3-4 minutes then stir in garlic. Add the celery and mushrooms and cook for 7-10 minutes until soft and the mushrooms have emitted most of their liquid.

Add the sage, stock, salt, pepper, butter, and quinoa and give it a good mix. Reduce heat to low, cover, and cook for around 5 minutes. If after 5 minutes the stuffing is very runny, increase the heat and allow the water to evaporate with the lid off for a couple of minutes.

Let the stuffing rest for 5-10 minutes before stirring in the pine nuts and serving.

ROASTED CAULIFLOWER & SPROUTS

These wonderful winter vegetables are enhanced with rosemary and garlic to really bring out the beautiful flavors. You can mix everything together in an oven proof dish the night before and leave in the fridge for the flavors to marinate. Just pop it into the oven 40 minutes before you plan to serve.

Preparation Time
10 minutes

Total Time
40 minutes

Makes
4 servings

INGREDIENTS

1.5oz / 50g pine nuts
1 large head of cauliflower
10.5oz / 300g brussel sprouts
3 cloves garlic, thinly sliced
2 tbsp olive oil
2 sprigs rosemary, chopped
½ tsp salt
½ tsp pepper

DIRECTIONS

Heat a medium pan and dry fry the pine nuts for 1-2 minutes until golden brown. Be sure to move them around constantly as they burn very quickly. Remove from heat and set aside.

Cut the cauliflower into small florets. Trim the ends from the Brussels sprouts and slice in half.

Place the cauliflower florets and sprouts in a large roasting pan, scatter over the rosemary and garlic, and drizzle over the olive oli. Season and mix together gently.

Roast in the oven for 25–30 minutes, until tender and beginning to brown on the edges, giving it a good mix half way through.

Transfer to a serving plate and scatter over pine nuts, then serve immediately.

ROASTED BEETROOTS

WITH ORANGE BALSAMIC GLAZE

The recipe features juicy ruby red sweet beetroots that have been oven roasted to perfection, with the addition of a tart balsamic glaze and delicate orange flavor.

Preparation Time
10 minutes

Total Time
1 hour

Makes
4-6 servings

INGREDIENTS

4 large beetroots, scrubbed &
top removed
½ cup balsamic vinegar
1 tbsp maple syrup
1 tsp grated orange
Salt and pepper, to taste

DIRECTIONS

Preheat the oven to 350°.

Individually wrap each beetroot in foil and bake in the oven for 50-55 minutes or until tender when pierced with a fork. Once cooked unwrap foil and leave to cool down.

While the beets are cooling heat the vinegar, maple syrup and orange zest in a small saucepan over medium heat. Bring to a boil then reduce to a simmer and allow to cook for 2-3 minutes until the sauce has thickened and reduced.

Once the beets have cooled down peel the skin off using a vegetable peeler then slice into ¼ -inch round slices.

Layer the beet slices on a large servings dish, season with salt and pepper, then drizzle with balsamic glaze.

WINTER ROOT ROASTED VEGETABLES

WITH PINE NUTS

A wonderful medley of colorful root vegetables that makes a versatile side dish. It's important to cut the vegetables evenly so they roast at the same rate. Oven roasting brings out the sweetness of the vegetables and seals in the flavor.

Preparation Time	**Total Time**	**Makes**
10 minutes	24 minutes	4-6 servings

INGREDIENTS

2 medium beetroots, peeled & cubed

3 medium carrots, cut into large chunks

1 red onion, peeled and cut into wedges

2 parsnips, peeled & cut into 1" pieces

1 turnip, ends cut off & cut into 1" pieces

8 new potatoes, halved lengthwise

3 tbsp olive oil

½ cup pine nuts, lightly toasted

¼ cup pumpkin seeds, lightly toasted

½ tsp coarse salt

¼ tsp black pepper

DIRECTIONS

Preheat oven to 350°.

Place all vegetables in a large bowl and evenly coat with olive oil then sprinkle with salt and pepper.

Transfer to a baking tray in a single layer. You may need to use two baking trays as you do not want to overcrowd each tray.

Roast vegetables in the oven for around 35 minutes, moving them around with a wooden spoon every 10-15 minutes to evenly cook them and ensure they do not stick to the pan.

Remove from the oven and transfer to a large serving bowl. Top with toasted pine nuts and pumpkin seeds and drizzle with balsamic dressing. Leave to cool to room temperature if serving cold, or serve immediately while warm.

Drizzle with balsamic vinegar if desired.

BRAISED RED CABBAGE WITH APPLES

A great accompaniment to a festive main dish that is jam packed with flavor. This side dish can be made up to two days ahead, making your Christmas meal prep a little easier.

Preparation Time
15 minutes

Total Time
1 hour

Makes
6-8 servings

INGREDIENTS

1 medium red cabbage
2 cooking apples, sliced
½ cup dried cranberries
1 tbsp brown sugar
3 tbsp apple cider vinegar
1 cinnamon stick
1 tsp of nutmeg
2 tbsp vegan butter
¼ tsp salt
¼ tsp pepper

DIRECTIONS

Peel away the outer layers of the cabbage then slice into quarters. Remove and discard the inner hard core then finely chop or shred the cabbage.

Add the butter to a pot or frying pan along with the apples, cinnamon stick, and cranberries. Cook over low heat for 5 minutes or until the apple has softened. Add the cabbage, sugar, vinegar, nutmeg, salt, and pepper. Place the lid on and cook over medium-low for 1 hour, checking occasionally to see if the mixture needs a dash of water and to give it a quick stir.

If the mixture is a little liquidy after an hour, remove the lid and cook over medium heat until the excess liquid has evaporated.

This dish is great served hot or cold.

CINNAMON ROASTED SWEET POTATOES & CRANBERRIES

A great festive twist on a classic Christmas table staple. The beautifully spiced flavors compliment the sweetness of the potato. Not only will this dish also add a vibrant splash of color to your table but you can prepare it in just 5 minutes.

Preparation Time
5 minutes

Total Time
45 minutes

Makes
4-6 servings

INGREDIENTS

6 cups / 1 kg sweet potatoes, diced
8 oz / 225g cranberries
1 tbsp vegan butter (or canola oil)
1 tbsp maple syrup
2 tsp cinnamon
1 tsp coarse salt

DIRECTIONS

Preheat the oven to 400°.

Place all ingredients in a large bowl and mix very well until everything is evenly mixed and the potatoes are coated in the cinnamon, maple, and salt.

Spread in an even layer on a baking sheet that has been lined with parchment paper and roast for 45-50 minutes or until tender and crisp on the outside. Sprinkle with a dash more salt before serving.

GARLIC & HERB POTATO GRATIN

If you have a large number of people to cook for over the holidays this recipe makes a fantastic dish that is elegant and luxurious, and hugely popular. The thinly sliced potatoes are layered along with bursts of garlic and herbs and roasted to crispy perfection.

Preparation Time	**Total Time**	**Makes**
15 minutes	1 hour 15 minutes	4 servings

INGREDIENTS

1.5lbs / 650g potatoes (Desiree or Yukon), peeled & cut into ¼" slices
4 cloves garlic, roughly chopped
2 tbsp freshly chopped herbs (parsley, rosemary, thyme, chives)
1.5 oz / 50ml olive oil
1 tbsp nutritional yeast

150ml / ⅔ cup vegetable stock (made with boiling water)
½ tsp salt
½ tsp pepper

DIRECTIONS

Rinse the potato slices to remove excess starch and drain them as well as you can, patting dry with a kitchen towel.

Place in a bowl along with all other ingredients except the stock. Mix well to ensure each potato is coated with oil.

Using an 8-inch oven dish layer the potatoes neatly on their sides (vertically) and pour the hot stock over. Place in the microwave on high for 10 minutes.

While the potatoes are in the microwave preheat the oven to 350°.

Bake in the oven for around 50 minutes or until the top is golden brown and crisp, and the potatoes are soft and tender.

PERFECT ROAST POTATOES

In our humble opinion roast potatoes are the best part of a Christmas meal! Super crispy on the outside and fluffy and moist on the inside, these really are the star piece at the table. If you are looking for the ultimate roast potato recipe then look no further!

Preparation Time	Total Time	Makes
10 minutes	1 hour 10 minutes	4 servings

INGREDIENTS

2.2lbs / 1kg roasting potatoes (Maris Piper or Yukon), peeled & cut evenly into either halves or quarters
¼ cup / 60ml olive oil
2 tsp all purpose flour
2 tsp sea salt

DIRECTIONS

Preheat the oven to 400°.

Place oil in a large roasting tray and heat in the oven, one large enough to fit all potatoes in a single layer. If you do not have one that is large enough then use two and evenly distribute the oil.

Put potatoes and 1 tsp salt in a large pot and fill with water to just cover. Place over the heat and allow the water to come to a boil. Once boiling reduce the heat to a vigorous simmer and cook for 2 minutes.

Drain your potatoes in a sieve and give them a good shake to fluff up the outsides. You want the outside of the potato to break away a little as this is the trick to getting them super crispy. Evenly sprinkle over the flour and give them another shake.

Carefully take the hot baking trays out of the oven and drop a potatoes into the oil. You want to hear it sizzle as it touches the oil. If you don't hear the sizzle just pop the pan back in the oven for a few more minutes to increase the temperature of the oil otherwise place all potatoes on the tray and ensure they are evenly coated.

Roast the potatoes for 20 minutes then take them out of the oven and turn each potato, then repeat this again after another 20 minutes. Roast for a further 10-20 minutes so they will have been in the oven for around one hour. Once they are looking crisp and golden take them out, sprinkle over 1 tsp salt and serve immediately.

YORKSHIRE PUDDINGS

A Christmas meal wouldn't be complete without these wonderful little puddings. Commonly made with milk and eggs, this vegan recipe could seriously rival any dairy based version.

| **Preparation Time** | **Total Time** | **Makes** |
| 5 minutes | 20 minutes | 4 servings |

INGREDIENTS

1 cup all-purpose flour
1 heaped tbsp gram/
chickpea flour
1 tsp baking powder
1 cup unsweetened dairy-
free milk
Vegetable oil, for greasing
¼ tsp coarse salt
¼ tsp freshly ground black
pepper

DIRECTIONS

Preheat the oven to 440°.

Once the oven is hot pour 1 tsp of vegetable oil in each hole of a metal muffin baking tin and place in the pre-heated oven for around 5-6 minutes or until it just starts smoking.

In a large bowl whisk together both flours, baking powder, salt, and pepper. Slowly add non-dairy milk, whisking well until fully combined and lump-free. Bubbles should start to form on the surface and the batter should be thin.

Carefully remove the oiled tin from the oven. Using a ladle or large spoon pour the batter into the moulds, filling only halfway up.

Transfer muffin tin back into the oven and bake for 15 minutes without opening the oven door, as this will prevent them from rising.

Serve immediately while hot and fluffy.

NO–BUTTER PUFF PASTRY

This genius recipe produces a wonderfully flaky and puffy pastry that can rival any version made with butter. The pastry freezes well so it's worth making extra and keeping a batch in your freezer for sweet or savory pies.

Preparation Time
10 minutes
(+ 30 minutes to
chill dough)

Total Time
30 minutes

Makes
1 lb

INGREDIENTS

2 cups all-purpose flour,
sieved
1 tbsp granulated sugar (for
sweet pies only)
½ tsp coarse salt
1 cup or 16 tbsp solid
coconut oil
¼ cup ice water
3 tbs soy milk

DIRECTIONS

Mix together flour, sugar, and salt in a large bowl. Slowly add 2 tablespoons of solid coconut oil at a time using two forks to mix. Continue to add remaining coconut oil until the mixture is crumbly and looks like small pea sized balls.

Add 2 tablespoons of ice water and mix in using your hands then add the soy milk and lemon juice, gently kneading, while continuing to add the water, 2 tablespoons at a time. The dough should be firm and hold together when pressed in between two fingers, but still have a crumbly texture.

Transfer the dough to a clean surface and knead using your hands for around 30 seconds. If the dough is too sticky add more flour, 1 teaspoon at a time, until it starts to come together.

Using a knife or spatula shape the dough into a rectangle, around 15x10", cover with plastic wrap and leave to chill in the fridge for 30 minutes.

Remove from the fridge and place on a lightly floured work surface.

Roll the dough out into a thin sheet then fold into thirds using three folds, lengthwise. Then rotate the dough 180 degrees on the work surface and fold it three times again so it becomes a thick square.

Roll the dough out again into a rectangle, around 6x5-inches and repeat the process until you are left with a thick square. The dough should be much smoother and elastic at this stage. You can either wrap the dough tightly in plastic wrap and freeze for later use or use in a recipe.

The dough is best when baked at 350° and brushed with soy milk before going into the oven.

HOMEMADE TRADITIONAL GRAVY

Rich and full of flavor, this gravy is perfect to accompany pies, a vegan meatloaf or even drizzled over vegetables for a delicious and rich homemade flavor.

Preparation Time	**Total Time**	**Makes**
10 minutes	30 minutes	Makes just over 2 cups

INGREDIENTS

1 large onion, roughly chopped
2 garlic cloves, minced
2 medium carrots, chopped
2 celery sticks, chopped
2 bay leaves
2 sprigs of fresh thyme

2 tbsp all-purpose flour
1 tbsp brown sugar
1 tbsp tomato purée
1 tsp soy sauce
2 tbsp red wine vinegar
4 cups vegetable stock
Olive Oil

DIRECTIONS

Heat a glug of olive oil in a large saucepan and sauté onions for 1-2 minutes until soft, then add garlic and cook for another minute. Add carrots, celery, bay leaves and thyme and cook for 10-15 minutes until tender when pierced with a fork.

Stir in the flour and fry for a minute until smooth and lump-free. Add sugar, tomato puree, soy sauce and red wine vinegar.

Pour in stock and bring to a boil. Reduce to a simmer and cook uncovered for 10-15 minutes for the gravy to thicken.

Using a potato masher crush the carrots and celery a little to release flavor then strain through a sieve.

Serve while hot or allow to cool to room temperature and refrigerate for up to 5 days. Heat in a saucepan or in the microwave when re-using.

SLOW COOKED SPICED APPLE

& SULTANA CHUTNEY

What better way to prepare a Christmas dish than by throwing all the ingredients into your slow cooker in the morning and forgetting about it until you are ready to serve later that day. The tangy sweet flavors which have been marrying together for hours in the slow cooker are accentuated by warming festive spices.

Preparation Time
30 minutes

Total Time
6 hours 30 minutes

Makes
2-3 jars

INGREDIENTS

175ml / ¾ cup apple cider vinegar
½ cup / 100g soft brown sugar
¼ cup / 50g caster sugar
2.6lbs / 1.2kg cooking apples (approx 4 apples), peeled, cored & diced
1.5 oz / 50g sultanas
2 small white onions, finely sliced
2 shallots, finely sliced
½ tbsp freshly grated ginger or 1 tsp ground ginger
½ tsp cinnamon
½ tsp nutmeg
½ mixed spice
¼ tsp cayenne
1 tbsp lemon juice
¼ tsp salt

DIRECTIONS

Set the slow cooker on the highest setting.

Add the vinegar and sugar and give it a good stir until it is fully mix in and the sugar is starting to dissolve.

Stir in the rest of the ingredients, mixing well, then cover and cook for 6 hours.

Give the chutney a good stir every few hours. If the chutney appears to be a little liquidy after the 6 hours remove some of the liquid with a spoon and continue to cook for 30 minutes with the lid off to allow the excess to evaporate.

Transfer the chutney to a serving bowl or mason jars and allow to cool to room temperature before serving.

The chutney will keep for 4-5 weeks in a sealed jar in the fridge.

DESSERTS & TREATS

TRADITIONAL MINCE PIES

This crumbly fruit filled sweet pie is a true Christmas classic. They are best served warm out of the oven and drizzled with custard.

Preparation Time
20 minutes

Total Time
45 minutes

Makes
18 mince pies

INGREDIENTS

1 Package of vegan shortcrust pastry (room temperature)

FOR THE FILLING

Juice and zest from a large orange
1 cup sultanas or raisins
1 medium apple, grated
½ cup dried cranberries
½ cup dried mulberries
2 tsp cinnamon
1 tsp ground ginger
½ tsp nutmeg
½ tsp ground clove
1 tsp vanilla essence
1 tbsp maple syrup
¼ cup water
½ cup soy milk
½ cup icing sugar, sieved

DIRECTIONS

Preheat your oven to 400°.

Place filling ingredients in a pan with around ¼ cup of water and allow it to simmer on a low heat for 10 minutes. Add a dash more water if the mixture becomes too dry. Do not boil the mixture, keep it at a gentle heat. Remove from heat and set aside to cool.

Grease a muffin tray with vegan butter or coconut oil and set aside.

Roll the pastry out evenly to around ⅛ inch / 3mm thick then cut in half. Cut out 18 large circles and 18 slightly smaller circles using different sized cookie cutters.

Line each hole with the larger pastry circle, gently pressing the pastry into the edges and up against the sides. Fill each one with mince meat but be sure not to overfill - keep it below the pastry edge.

Slightly dampen the edges of the smaller pastry circle and press the lids on each pie, sealing the edges to ensure the filling will not leak.

Lightly brush each pie with soy milk then using a very sharp knife make two incisions on the top of the pie to allow steam to escape.

Bake in the oven for 22-25 minutes until lightly golden brown.

Sieve icing sugar on top as soon as they come out of the oven, then remove from muffin tin and allow to cool to room temperature.

ROASTED PECAN SHORTBREAD

Christmas just doesn't feel right without the buttery deliciousness of shortbread. This foolproof recipe tastes just like traditional shortbread and has the same crumbly texture as versions made with butter. Be sure to use a good quality vegan butter that you like the taste of as this will affect the flavour of your biscuits.

Preparation Time
10 minutes
(30 minutes chilling time)

Total Time
30 minutes

Makes
22 shortbread cookies

INGREDIENTS

¾ cup + 2 tbsp / 200g vegan butter (just above room temperature)
1 tsp vanilla essence
½ cup / 100g caster sugar
¼ tsp salt
2½ cups / 300g all-purpose flour, sifted
1 tbsp cornflour
2.5 oz / 80g pecans

DIRECTIONS

Heat the oven to 350°. Once heated place the pecans in a single layer on a baking tray and roast for 3-4 minutes. Keep an eye on the nuts while they are roasting as they will burn very quickly. Remove from the oven, roughly chop on a chopping board and set aside to cool.

Place butter and sugar in a bowl and cream for 3 minutes, scraping down the sides at least once. Add the vanilla and salt and mix again.

Add the flour in 3 batches, but be sure to whisk until just combined. Do not over mix the dough. Fold in the pecans.

Remove the dough from the bowl and give it a quick knead on a floured surface then wrap in plastic wrap and place in the fridge for 30-45 minutes.

Preheat the oven to 350°.

Roll the pastry out to approximately ¼ inch / ½ cm thick on a floured surface and use a cookie cutter to make shapes until you have used all the pastry.

Place on a lined baking tray and sprinkle each cookie with a little white sugar.

Bake for 20 minutes or until golden brown.

Cool on a cooling rack for at least 10 minutes before eating.

SALTED CARAMEL APPLE PIE

This mouth-watering recipe turns out a beautifully flaky and delicious homemade pie crust, that is surprisingly quick and easy to make. Soft and tender apples are drenched in a perfectly balanced salted caramel, making a warm and comforting dessert that is delicious served with vanilla ice cream.

Preparation Time	**Total Time**	**Makes**
25 minutes	1 hour 10 minutes	8 servings

INGREDIENTS

FOR THE CARAMEL SAUCE

$\frac{1}{3}$ cup / 80ml coconut oil
$\frac{1}{3}$ cup / 80ml maple syrup
2 $\frac{1}{2}$ tbsp almond butter
$\frac{1}{8}$ tsp sea salt

FOR THE PASTRY

2$\frac{1}{2}$ cups / 350g all-purpose flour
2 tbsp caster sugar
$\frac{1}{4}$ tsp salt
1 cup / 225g cold vegan butter
$\frac{1}{3}$ cup / 80ml ice cold water

FOR THE APPLE PIE FILLING

2.2 lbs / 1kg cooking apples
1 tbsp freshly squeezed lemon juice
$\frac{1}{4}$ tsp ground cloves
$\frac{1}{4}$ tsp ground nutmeg
1 $\frac{1}{2}$ tsp ground cinnamon
1 tbsp cornstarch

DIRECTIONS

FOR THE PASTRY

Place flour, sugar and vegan butter in your food processor and process until it resembles fine breadcrumbs. Add one tablespoon at a time of ice cold water and pulse until the dough starts to come together. Try not to add too much water as it will make the dough chewy rather than light and flakey.

Remove the dough from the food processor once it has clumped together (over-working it can make the pastry too tough) and place on a sheet of plastic wrap. Shape the dough into a ball, cover with the plastic wrap and leave to chill in the fridge for 30 minutes.

FOR THE SALTED CARAMEL:

While the dough is chilling make the caramel sauce by placing coconut oil and maple syrup in a small heavy bottomed saucepan over low heat. Once the coconut oil has melted add almond butter and whisk for 30 seconds until fully incorporated and smooth, then add salt. Remove from the heat and set aside.

FOR THE FILLING:

Preheat the oven to 340° and grease a 9-inch pie dish with a thin layer of melted coconut oil.

Peel the apples and chop them into approx ¼ -inch / ½ cm slices. Place the apples in a large saucepan with the lemon juice, spices and cornstarch, and mix well to combine.

Let the apples cook for 4-5 minutes over medium heat, stirring frequently to prevent them from sticking to the bottom. You want the apples to slightly soften but not fully cook.

Remove from the heat and stir in ¾ of the caramel sauce, mixing well. Set aside.

TO MAKE THE PIE:

Remove the dough from the fridge and divide in two.

Roll out one half so that it is large enough to cover the surface and sides of the pastry dish. Line the dish, gently pressing the pastry into the edges. Pour in the apple filling, smoothing over the top so that it is as flat as possible.

Roll out the second half of the pastry and using a pizza cutter or a sharp knife cut ½-inch wide strips for the lattice top. Weave the strips over and under each other, starting with 4-5 parallel strips to get you started then threading one strip perpendicular to the parallel strip and weaving it over and under. Continue this process until you have completed the lattice top.

Trim the sides and any overhanging pastry and brush the top with a thin layer of the remaining caramel sauce.

Bake for 35 minutes until golden brown. Check the pie after 20 minutes and cover the sides or top with foil if it looks like it is browning too quickly.

Remove from the oven and leave to cool for an hour before serving.

Serve with any leftover caramel sauce and vegan vanilla ice cream if desired.

CRISP CHRISTMAS SUGAR COOKIES

These light, crisp and yummy cookies are a family favorite at Christmas, and with a total time of 20 minutes how can you resists whipping up a batch (or two!) over the holidays.

Preparation Time
10 minutes

Total Time
20 minutes

Makes
20 cookies

INGREDIENTS

1 cup coconut oil, room temperature
½ cup aquafaba (liquid from 1 can chickpeas)
1 cup caster sugar
1 ½ tsp vanilla extract
2 tsp baking powder
3 cups all-purpose flour, sifted
½ tsp salt

DIRECTIONS

Preheat oven to 350°.

Line a baking sheet with parchment paper. Set aside.

In a large bowl sift flour, baking powder, and salt and set aside.

Add sugar and coconut oil together and cream for 3-4 minutes, scraping the sides down as you go along.

Mix flour into the sugar/oil mixture in 3 batches until just incorporated, making sure to not overmix.

Place dough onto a floured surface and knead a few times.

Roll the dough out to ¼ inch thickness and do not worry if it is a little crumbly.

Cut cookies with cookie cutter and place on baking tray.

Bake in the oven for no longer than 10 minutes. Do not leave them in too long otherwise they will not hold together and you will be unable to ice them.

Cool on a cooling rack for at least 30 minutes before icing.

GINGERBREAD COOKIES

These adorable gingerbread men make for a lovely Christmas present, as well as a tasty treat for a winter's afternoon. Fill your home with the most delicious aroma of these traditional crisp spiced gingerbread cookies baking in the oven.

Preparation Time	**Total Time**	**Makes**
15 minutes (+ 2 hours for the dough to chill)	30 minutes	24 gingerbread cookies

INGREDIENTS

2 cups whole wheat flour
1 tsp baking powder
½ tsp baking soda
2 tsp ground ginger
1 tsp cinnamon
½ tsp ground cloves
¼ tsp mixed spice or pumpkin spice
½ tsp salt

½ cup dark brown sugar
¼ cup coconut oil, softened (but not melted)
¼ cup molasses
¼ cup unsweetened applesauce
1 tsp vanilla extract
2 tbsp non-dairy milk

DIRECTIONS

In a large bowl, whisk flour, baking powder, ginger, cinnamon, cloves, baking soda, baking powder and salt. Set aside.

Add sugar and coconut oil to a medium bowl and cream for 2-3 minutes using an electric whisk, scraping down the sides as you go along.

Add molasses, applesauce, vanilla and milk and continue to whisk for another minute.

Pour the sugar mixture into the flour and use a wooden spoon to gently mix until the dough comes together. Add 1 tbsp more flour if the dough seems too sticky.

Turn dough out onto a floured work surface and knead for a minute until the dough is smooth. Wrap the dough in plastic wrap and refrigerate for 2-4 hours, preferably overnight.

Preheat the oven to 350°. Line a baking tray with parchment paper.

Lightly flour a work surface and knead the dough for around 30 seconds. Roll the dough out to about ¼ inch thick and use a gingerbread-man shaped cookie cutter to cut the dough until you have finished it all.

Place on baking tray and bake for 14-16 minutes until golden brown.

Wait for the gingerbread cookies to cool down completely before icing.

CHRISTMAS BROWNIES

These festive brownies are a real treat for any chocoholic! The rich dark chocolate flavor is complimented by a fruity mince pie filling as well as crunchy walnuts. A wonderful indulgent treat that also makes a great homemade gift.

Preparation Time
10 minutes

Total Time
40 minutes

Makes
16 slices of brownie

INGREDIENTS

2oz / 60g dairy free butter
4.2oz / 120g vegan milk chocolate
2.6oz / 75g vegan dark chocolate
2 tbsp golden syrup
2oz / 60g vegan biscuits (Graham Crackers / Digestives etc)

2oz / 60g vegan mini marshmallows
2oz / 60g Sweet n Salty popcorn
1.7oz / 50g brazil or macadamia nuts, roughly chopped
2 tbsps glace cherries, chopped

DIRECTIONS

Line a brownie tin with parchment paper

In a medium heatproof bowl melt the butter, all the chocolate and the syrup over a bain marie, stirring frequently. Keep an eye on it as the chocolate is prone to burning. Remove from the heat once the ingredients have fully incorporated.

Place the biscuits in a freezer bag and gently bash them to create small pieces - some of which are crushed.

Fold the biscuits into the chocolate mixture along with the

marshmallows, popcorn, nuts and cherries. Pour into the brownie tin and smooth the top by pressing down very gently then chill in the fridge for a minimum of 4 hours to set.

Remove from the fridge and slice into squares. Store in an airtight container for up to 5 days.

Bake for 27-30 minutes or until a toothpick comes out clean.

Leave in the tin for 10 minutes then remove and transfer to a cooling rack before slicing into squares.

THE ULTIMATE POPCORN ROCKY ROAD

This no bake wonder is stuffed with vegan marshmallows, brazil nuts and popcorn to create a sweet, salty, chewy and crunchy treat that is sure to please friends and family alike. The combination of using vegan milk and dark chocolate creates the perfect balance of chocolatey goodness!

Preparation Time
10 minutes

Total Time
4 hours 10 minutes

Makes
12 bars

INGREDIENTS

¾ cup glutinous rice flour, sieved
2 heaped tbsp sugar
⅓ cup water, boiling
Pinch of salt
1 tsp baking powder
1 tbsp vegetable oil

3.5oz / 100g sweetened red bean paste or lotus paste
¼ cup white sesame seeds
1 ½ cups vegetable oil, for frying

DIRECTIONS

In a medium bowl mix rice flour, sugar, and salt together. Add boiling water and mix well until you have a rough dough, then add vegetable oil.

Transfer to a kitchen surface lightly dusted with glutinous rice flour and knead for a few minutes until the oil has completely absorbed.

Roll the dough out into a thin 'log' and cut it into 8 equal pieces. Roll each ball out into a 'disk' then spoon ½-1 teaspoon of the red bean paste into the middle. Seal completely - ensuring there are no gaps for the red bean paste to leak then shape into a round ball.

Heat vegetable oil in a wok over medium heat. It needs to reach around 210-250°c.

Prepare two bowls, one with water and one with sesame seeds. Quickly dip each ball into the water to lightly coat it, then dip it in the sesame seeds and gently roll it in between the palms of your hands to ensure the sesame seeds stick. Continue with remaining balls.

Carefully place balls into the hot oil (you may need to do this in batches to not overcrowd the pan) and slowly deep fry for 5 minutes, without touching or moving the balls as the sesame seeds may drop off. After 5 minutes gently turn the balls over using a metal tong.

The balls will initially stay at the bottom of the pan, then slowly float to the surface of the oil. Once they start to float use the metal tongs or a pair of chopsticks to continuously submerge the balls in the hot oil and gently press them against the sides of the wok. You will see the balls expanding in size once you start to press them against the sides. Try to press each ball evenly on each side to ensure you are left with a round shape.

Once the balls have expanded to around 3 times the size they were originally and they have browned a little you can remove them from the heat using a slotted spoon and transfer to a paper towel lined plate.

Allow to cool a little but serve while warm and crisp.

It is recommended that sesame balls are eaten on they day they are made as they do not keep particularly well the following day.

GINGERBREAD SPICED PANCAKES WITH MAPLE PECAN DRIZZLE

A festive twist on a staple recipe that can be enjoyed for breakfast, lunch or even a lazy dinner... after all Christmas is for allowing yourself to indulge a little! They are wonderfully fluffy and are perfect drizzled with maple pecan topping.

Preparation Time	**Total Time**	**Makes**
10 minutes	20 minutes	6-8 Pancakes

INGREDIENTS

FOR THE PANCAKES

1 cup all-purpose flour
1 tbsp gingerbread spice
2 tbsp dark brown sugar
1 tbsp baking powder
¼ tsp coarse salt
1 cup non-dairy milk
1 tsp vanilla essence

FOR THE TOPPING

½ cup maple syrup
1 tbsp ginger preserves
2 tbsp roasted pecan nuts, chopped

DIRECTIONS

In a large bowl sieve flour, spices, and baking powder. Add sugar and salt and mix well.

Whisk in milk and vanilla and leave for 2-3 minutes for the baking powder to activate.

In the meantime prepare the topping my mixing all ingredients together, then set aside.

Grease a large frying pan with vegetable oil or vegan butter and heat over medium heat for 1-2 minutes until the pan is hot. Give the batter a quick whisk to ensure no lumps have developed then, using a ladle, spoon approx. ¼ cup of batter onto the pan.

Decrease the heat to medium-low. Flip only once when small bubbles start to appear, around 1-2 minutes on each side. Depending on the size of your frying pan you may be able to cook more than one pancake at a time.

Serve immediately with the maple pecan topping drizzled over the top.

GINGERBREAD DOUGHNUTS WITH ORANGE-MAPLE GLAZE

These deliciously fluffy baked doughnuts are made with oat and almond flour, and perfectly spiced with festive cinnamon, ginger, cloves and nutmeg. They are as good as the real thing and much healthier too!

Preparation Time	**Total Time**	**Makes**
15 minutes	40 minutes	12 doughnuts

INGREDIENTS

FOR THE DOUGHNUTS

2 tbsp ground flaxseed
1 cup / 120g oat flour*
1 cup / 100g almond flour
1 tsp baking powder
1 tsp cinnamon
½ tsp ginger
¼ tsp nutmeg
½ tsp salt
4 tbsp coconut sugar
4 tbsp agave nectar
4 tbsp coconut oil, melted
4 tbsp dairy free milk

1 tsp vanilla essence
4 tbsp cashew butter (or other nut butter)

FOR THE ORANGE MAPLE GLAZE

1 cup powdered sugar, sieved
1 tbsp maple syrup
2 tbsp dairy free milk
¼ tsp apple cider vinegar
1 tbsp orange zest

*You can make your own oat flour by pulsing oats in a food processor until a fine powder has formed.

DIRECTIONS

To start, make the flax 'egg' by combining 2 tablespoons of ground flaxseeds with 6 tablespoons of water. Mix well then leave to thicken for at least 10 minutes while you prepare the doughnuts.

Prepare a doughnut mould by lightly greasing it with a thin layer of coconut oil or vegan butter.

Combine both flours, baking powder, sugar, spices and salt in a large bowl and mix well.

In a separate bowl combine agave nectar, coconut oil, dairy free milk, vanilla, and cashew butter and mix until the cashew butter has fully incorporated. Add the flax mixture then pour into the dry mix, stirring with a wooden spoon until combined.

Divide the mixture evenly into the greased donut tray, filling each mould ¾ of the way up as they will rise when baking.

Bake for 25 minutes. Remove from the oven and leave to cool for 20 minutes before gently removing them from the mould with a sharp knife.

TO MAKE THE GLAZE:

Combine the icing sugar and maple syrup in a small bowl, whisking until combined. Add a tablespoon of dairy free milk and ¼ tsp apple cider vinegar and whisk again. You want the glaze to be thick, smooth and glossy, and you may be able to achieve this with just one tablespoon of milk. Add a dash more if it is too thick but make sure to not add too much liquid or it will be runny. Stir in the orange zest and set aside.

Dip each cooled doughnut into the glaze to cover the top half and transfer to a wire rack for the glaze to set. You can place paper towels under the wire rack to catch any excess glaze that may drip.

CHRISTMAS CHEESECAKE

This luxurious, creamy and sweet cheesecake makes a great Christmas dessert and is impossible to resist! Don't let the word 'cheese' fool you, this dessert is free of cholesterol, animal fat, and is 100% vegan.

Preparation Time
10 minutes
(+ 1 hour to soak cashews)

Total Time
4 hours 15 minutes
(incl. 4 hrs to set)

Makes
12 slices

INGREDIENTS

FOR THE CRUST

1 cup / 130g raw almonds
1 cup / 130g raisins
2 tbsp full-fat coconut milk

FOR THE FILLING

1¼ cup / 200g raw cashews
½ cup coconut oil, melted
¼ cup maple syrup
½ cup full-fat coconut milk
¼ cup lemon juice
1 tsp vanilla extract

FOR THE TOPPING

½ cup cranberries, fresh or frozen
2 tbsp chia seeds
1 tsp vanilla extract
1 tsp caster sugar
1 tsp mixed spice (or pumpkin spice mix)
½ cup roasted slivered almonds

DIRECTIONS

Place the cashew nuts in a heatproof bowl and pour boiling water over them until just covered. Cover the bowl and leave to soak for 1 hour.

Prepare a springform pie tin, or use a standard pie tin and line with parchment paper.

While the cashews are soaking place the raisins in a separate heatproof bowl and cover with room temperature water. Leave to soak for 45 minutes.

Once the raisins have finished soaking drain them well and pat dry with a kitchen towel. Place in a food processor or blender and blend until they have completely broken down and form a ball. Remove and set aside.

Place the almonds in the blender (you do not need to wash the blender after pulsing the raisins) and blend until it resembles fine breadcrumbs. Do not blend too much or the almonds will start to become a paste. Add the raisins and coconut milk and blend until fully incorporated.

Transfer the crust into the pie tin and press down using the back of a spoon to even it out. Cover loosely with plastic wrap and place in the freezer while you prepare the filling.

Drain the cashew nuts. In a clean blender place all of the filling ingredients and blend until completely smooth and creamy with no lumps or solids.

Remove crust from the freezer and pour in the filling, evening out the top with a pallet knife or the back of a spoon. Return to the freezer for 4 hours to set.

Next, make the cranberry jam by placing the cranberries in a bowl and using a fork or potato masher to mash them up and squeeze the juice out. Add the chia seeds, sugar, vanilla, and spices. Mix well, then place in the fridge for half an hour.

Remove the cheesecake at least 15 minutes before you intend to serve it in order for it to defrost.

As soon as you remove it from the freezer and while it is still solid, spread the jam in an even layer over the top then sprinkle with slivered almonds.

The cheesecake will keep for 3-4 days in the fridge or 1 month in the freezer.

GINGERBREAD CUPCAKES WITH ORANGE SPICED BUTTERCREAM FROSTING

These irresistible cupcakes are moist, warmly spiced and come with a huge dollop of mouthwatering buttercream frosting. These truly are the perfect cupcakes to get you in a festive mood.

Preparation Time
20 minutes

Total Time
45 minutes

Makes
12 cupcakes

INGREDIENTS

DRY INGREDIENTS:

1½ cups all-purpose flour
½ cup soft brown
1 tsp baking soda
1 tsp ground cinnamon
½ tsp ground ginger
½ tsp ground nutmeg
¼ tsp ground cloves
¼ cup raisins or sultanas
2 tbsp flaked or desiccated coconut
½ tsp salt

WET INGREDIENTS:

½ cup molasses
½ cup non-dairy
⅓ cup canola oil
2 tbsp apple cider vinegar
1 tbsp vanilla extract

FROSTING:

½ cup vegan butter, room temperature
½ cup vegetable shortening
Zest from ½ an orange
2½ cups icing sugar
¼ cup molasses
1½ tsp salt
1 tsp vanilla extract
1 tsp cinnamon
½ tsp ginger
½ tsp nutmeg
¼ tsp ground cloves
1 tsp brandy or bourbon (optional)
1 tbsp nondairy milk (if needed to thin)

DIRECTIONS

TO MAKE THE CUPCAKES:

Preheat the oven to 350°. Line a cupcake tray with cupcake liners.

Mix all dry ingredients together in a large bowl.

Whisk all wet ingredients together in a separate large bowl.

Pour the wet ingredients into the dry and use a spatula to fold the ingredients into each other until just combined, making sure to not overmix.

Spoon the batter evenly into each cupcake liner and bake for 22-25 minutes until a toothpick comes out clean. Remove from the oven and allow the muffins to cool down to room temperature before frosting.

TO MAKE THE FROSTING:

Cream the butter and shortening in a large bowl using a stand mixer or electric whisk for 2 minutes. Add the icing sugar in ½ cup increments, scraping down the sides as you go along. This process should take around 5-6 minutes to get the frosting really creamy. Add all other ingredients and whisk for a minute.

SUGAR–FREE FESTIVE FRUIT CAKE

Who can resist a rich thick slice of delicious fruit cake? This gluten-free and refined sugar-free recipe is packed with fruit, nuts, and spices and is sure to become a firm family favorite. You certainly won't have to feel guilty asking for a second slice of this cake!

Preparation Time
10 minutes
(+12 hours to soak fruit)

Total Time
2 hours

Makes
1 large fruit cake

INGREDIENTS

2 lb / 900g mixed dried fruit
2 ½ cups / 570ml non-dairy milk
¾ cup / 200ml coconut oil
1 lb / 455g self-raising wholemeal flour
2 oz / 55g ground almonds
¼ cup walnuts, chopped

½ tsp cinnamon
1 tbsp molasses
1 tsp vanilla essence
Zest of ½ lemon
Zest of ½ orange
10 glazed cherries, chopped
¼ tsp salt

DIRECTIONS

Start by placing the fruit in a heatproof bowl and pouring boiling water over to cover completely. Cover the bowl with a plate so the steam cannot escape and leave to soak for 12-24 hours.

Preheat the oven to 300°.

Add all ingredients together and mix very well until fully combined, scraping down the sides as you go along.

Transfer to a loaf tin, smoothing the top with the back of a spoon. Bake for 1 hour at 300° then reduce the heat to 250° and bake for another hour.

CRANBERRY, APPLE & GINGERBREAD CRUMBLE

You can't beat a comforting crumble served piping hot out of the oven with a scoop of ice cream. This recipe is the ultimate quick and easy dessert that you can throw together in no time and makes the perfect treat.

Preparation Time
10 minutes

Total Time
25 minutes

Makes
6 servings

INGREDIENTS

FOR THE FILLING

2-3 apples (approx 10.5 oz / 300g), peeled & chopped
1 cup / 150g cranberries
1 tbsp brown sugar
3 tbsp water
1 tsp vanilla essence

FOR THE CRUMBLE

1½ cups / 150g almond flour
3 tbsp canola oil
1 tsp blackstrap molasses
1 tbsp brown sugar
1½ tsp ground ginger
¼ tsp cinnamon
1 tsp mixed spice
⅛ tsp salt

DIRECTIONS

Preheat oven to 350°.

Add the fruit, brown sugar and water to a saucepan. Bring the mixture to a simmer and cook for 8-10 minutes until the fruit has softened and the mixture has thickened. Remove from the heat and spoon into an ovenproof baking dish, then set aside.

In a large bowl add the almond flour, molasses, sugar, ginger, cinnamon, mixed spice and salt and mix well. Add in the oil, one tablespoon at a time, and mix by rubbing your fingers together.

The mixture should start to resemble coarse breadcrumbs.

Crumble the topping over the fruit evenly and bake in the oven for 8-10 minutes until the top is crisp and golden.

Serve while hot with custard or a scoop of ice cream.

FESTIVE SPICED FRUIT BAKE

This warm spiced mixture of fruit is such a versatile dish as you can substitute in any fruit you like. It can be served as a guilt free treat for breakfast, lunch or dinner. The most popular way to serve this is piping hot out of the oven with whipped coconut cream, ice cream or custard.

| **Preparation Time** | **Total Time** | **Makes** |
| 10 minutes | 1 hour 10 minutes | 5 Servings |

INGREDIENTS

2 cup cooking apples, sliced
2 cups peaches, fresh or canned
1 ½ cup fresh cranberries
1 cup pineapple chunks from a can (save the juice)
1 tbsp lemon juice
4 tbsp vegan butter, melted
⅓ cup brown sugar or coconut sugar
1 tbsp maple syrup or agave nectar
1 tsp cinnamon
¼ tsp nutmeg
2 tbsp coconut oil, melted
1 tsp vanilla extract
⅓ cup mixed nuts, chopped

DIRECTIONS

Preheat oven to 300° F.

Place all fruit in a large bowl and mix together with lemon juice, ensuring each piece of fruit is coated. Set aside.

In a separate bowl combine melted butter, sugar, spices, oil, vanilla and 1-2 tbsp of leftover pineapple juice.

Pour this liquid mixture over the fruit and give it a good stir to evenly coat.

Transfer to an ovenproof baking dish and bake for 1 hour, removing after 30 minutes to add nuts and give the mixture a stir.

Remove from the oven and add serve piping hot.

FESTIVE DRINKS

MULLED BLACKBERRY & VANILLA WINE

No Christmas is complete without a warming mug of mulled wine that is brimming with festive spices. This is mulled wine with a twist as blackberries are added for a delicious burst of flavor followed by a hint of sweet vanilla.

Preparation Time	**Total Time**	**Makes**
5 minutes	45 minutes	5-6 glasses

INGREDIENTS

11 oz / 330g blackberries (fresh or frozen)
1 ½ cups / 350ml apple juice (freshly juiced if possible)
1.7 oz / 50g white sugar
4 cloves
1 cinnamon stick
A few large peels of orange skin
1 vanilla pod, split open and scrape before adding the whole pod (or 1 tsp vanilla extract)
3 cups / 750ml bottle vegan red wine

DIRECTIONS

Add all ingredients except wine to a large pot and bring to a boil for 5-6 minutes until it starts to thicken and resemble a syrup.

Reduce to a low heat, pour in the red wine and simmer for 5-6 minutes until hot. Do not let the mixture boil.

Strain through a sieve and use the back of a spoon to push any juicy bits through the sieve.

Serve while hot.

YULETIDE MULLED MEAD

There's no better way to kick off the holiday season than with a warm pot of mulled mead heating over the stove. Cardamom, cinnamon, cloves, and orange are combined to create a wonderfully aromatic and comforting drink that will keep you warm on those cold winter nights.

Preparation Time
5 minutes

Total Time
10 minutes

Makes approx.
4 cups

INGREDIENTS

3 ¼ cups / 750ml mead or cider
2 tbsp brandy (optional)
1 cup / 250ml apple juice
1 strip of orange peel
3 cardamom pods
4 peppercorns
3 cloves
1 cinnamon stick
1-inch piece fresh ginger, sliced

DIRECTIONS

Place the spices and the piece of ginger in a cheesecloth, wrap them up and secure with an elastic band or twine.

Pour mead or cider into a saucepan along with the brandy, apple juice, orange peel and the spices and gently heat for 30 minutes, making sure to not boil the liquid.

Remove the spices and serve hot, garnished with a cinnamon stick if desired.

IRISH CREAM LIQUOR (HOMEMADE BAILEYS)

Christmas doesn't feel the same without a rich and creamy glass of Baileys Irish Cream, and now with this vegan version you can indulge in your favorite festive drink. This homemade version takes just 10 minutes to make and is much lighter and healthier than its dairy based counterpart so you can indulge-guilt free!

Preparation Time
10 minutes

Total Time
10 minutes

Makes approx.
2 ½ cups

INGREDIENTS

1 can (14 oz / 400ml) full-fat coconut milk
2-3 tbsp coconut or brown sugar
¼ - ⅓ cup / 60-75ml whiskey
¼ cup / 60ml strong fresh coffee
1 tsp vanilla essence

DIRECTIONS

Heat the coconut milk and sugar in a small saucepan over low heat, whisking well to ensure the sugar has dissolved. Allow the mixture to simmer for 10 minutes, stirring frequently, until it has thickened.

Pour in the whiskey (depending on how strong you like it!), coffee, and vanilla and heat for another minute, stirring constantly.

Remove from the heat and store in glass sealable jars.

Store in the fridge for up to two days, giving the mixture a good shake before serving as the coffee may settle at the bottom.

CREAMY CHRISTMAS EGGNOG

Christmas wouldn't be the same without this creamy indulgent drink to keep you warm in the winter. Enjoy this classic recipe with a twist, and the best part about it is that it's 100% vegan! This recipe produces a frothy, creamy and rich eggnog that is sure to get you feeling festive. Try to use freshly grated nutmeg as it makes a huge difference in flavor.

Preparation Time
5 minutes
(plus 4 hours for soaking & 1 hour to chill)

Total Time
7 minutes

Makes
5-6 cups

INGREDIENTS

2 cups water
1 can (14 oz / 400g) full-fat coconut milk
1 cup raw cashews
8 Medjool dates, pitted
1-2 tbsp brown sugar
½ tsp freshly grated nutmeg

½ tsp ground cinnamon
1 vanilla pod, use scrapings only or 1 tsp vanilla essence
⅛ tsp salt
⅛ tsp turmeric
2 shots whiskey or bourbon (optional)

DIRECTIONS

Place the dates and cashews in a heatproof bowl and pour hot water over them. Leave to soak for 4 hours, or preferably overnight.

Drain and place in a blender with all other ingredients, except whiskey. Blend for 1-2 minutes or until all ingredients are fully blended and smooth. Remove from blender and place in a sealed container. Add whiskey at this stage if using.

Chill in the fridge for at least one hour before serving.

RICH & CREAMY HOT CHOCOLATE

This recipe is a great way to curb any chocolate craving. The velvet smooth texture and rich chocolate flavor will keep you coming back to this recipe over and over again. Using simple ingredients and with a prep time of 10 minutes how could you resist!

Preparation Time
10 minutes

Total Time
30 minutes

Makes approx.
2 cups

INGREDIENTS

1 ½ tbsp caster sugar or agave nectar
3 tbsp cocoa powder
1 tsp arrowroot, tapioca or cornstarch
2 cups unsweetened non-dairy milk
1 tsp vanilla extract
Pinch of cinnamon
Pinch of sea salt

DIRECTIONS

Mix the sugar, cocoa, starch, salt and cinnamon together in a bowl.

Heat the milk gently over a low heat for 4-5 minutes, making sure it does not boil. Add the vanilla.

Whisk in 2 tablespoons of the milk into the cocoa-starch mixture and whisk until smooth then pour into the hot milk. Increase the heat and whisk constantly for 5 minutes until it thickens, ensuring the milk does not catch on the bottom of the saucepan.

Remove from heat and pour into cups. Allow to cool for a few minutes as it will be too hot to drink immediately.

SLOW COOKER SPICED LATTE

Warming festive spices combined with dairy free milk, vanilla and coffee creates a mug of deliciousness, that has been slowly cooking for hours. The flavors really intensify and deepen during the five hour cook. This recipe makes 6-8 large mugs of latte and can easily be doubled if you want to store it in the fridge and reheat another day.

Preparation Time	**Total Time**	**Makes approx.**
5 minutes	5 hours 5 minutes	6-8 cups

INGREDIENTS

6 cups non-dairy milk
¼ cup maple syrup or agave nectar
2 tbsp light brown sugar
1 tsp ground ginger
½ tsp ground cloves
½ tsp ground nutmeg

1 vanilla pod, scrapings and whole pod added or 1 tbsp vanilla extract
2 cinnamon sticks
2 ½ cups strongly brewed coffee

DIRECTIONS

Set your slow cooker to low.

Add all ingredient to the slow cooker and give it a good stir to thoroughly combine and dissolve the sugar as much as possible.

Cook for 5 hours, stirring every couple of hours or so and to check it has not started to boil. If it does turn your slow cooker to low for the remainder of it's cooking time.

Stir again before serving and enjoy with festive cookies, vegan marshmallows or coconut whipped cream.

MORE GREAT TITLES

· ·

HIGH CEDAR PRESS

CHECK OUT THE FULL COLLECTION!

CPSIA information can be obtained
at www.ICGtesting.com
Printed in the USA
LVHW081207090120
643062LV00017B/652/P

9 781979 578998